THE LETT

BY IVAN BULLOCH

Written by Diane James
Photography by Toby Maudsley

CONTENTS

SIMON & SCHUSTER BOOKS FOR YOUNG READERS

Simon & Schuster Building, Rockefeller Center, 1230 Avenue of the Americas, New York, New York 10020
Illustrations and design copyright © 1990 by Ivan Bulloch. Text and compilation copyright © 1990 by Two-Can Publishing Ltd. All rights reserved including the right of reproduction in whole or in part in any form. Originally published in Great Britain by Two-Can Publishing Ltd. First U.S. edition 1991. SIMON & SCHUSTER BOOKS FOR YOUNG READERS is a trademark of Simon & Schuster. Manufactured in Hong Kong.

10 9 8 7 6 5 4 3 2 1   (pbk.) 10 9 8 7 6 5 4 3 2 1

Library of Congress Cataloging-in-Publication Data: Bulloch, Ivan. The letter book / by Ivan Bulloch ; written by Diane James; photography by Toby Maudsley. Includes index. Summary: Suggests how to use the letters of the alphabet to create pictures, pop-ups, and other artistic patterns. 1. Alphabets—Juvenile literature. 2. Art—Technique—Juvenile literature. [1. Alphabets in art. 2. Art—Technique.] I. James, Diane. II. Maudsley, Toby, ill. III. Title. N7433.B8 1991 90-47117 745.6'1—dc20 CIP AC
ISBN 0-671-73886-0   ISBN 0-671-73887-9 (pbk.)

You do not need any special equipment to make or draw letters. In this book you will find out how to tear letters from colored paper, how to stencil and print letters and even how to make letters using food.

Look carefully at the shapes of letters in newspapers and magazines and make a collection of the letters you like best.

You will need to use a safety craft knife when cutting stencils, but always ask a grown-up for help.

paint

spray (for using with stencils)

paint dish

printing kit

flat brush

round brush

stencil brush

felt-tip pens

colored paper

sponge

eraser

T square

pencils

italic pen

safety craft knife

ruler

All the letters in the alphabet can be made from basic shapes such as circles, triangles, squares and rectangles. You can try this for yourself by cutting shapes from colored paper.

Most letters can be made using different combinations of shapes. See how many variations you can make of just one letter.

abcdef
ms
mir

Letters do not have to be formed perfectly with neat edges and round curves. Try tearing letters from colored paper so that they have a rough edge. Cut or tear small pieces of colored paper and use them to decorate your letters. When you have enough letters collected stick them on a piece of cardboard to make a letter picture.

All these letters were made from things you can probably find in your home.

We used building blocks, rope, straws, paper clips and modeling clay. Look for other things that could be used. Experiment with ways to make some letters lie flat and others stand up.

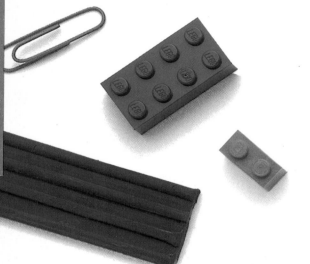

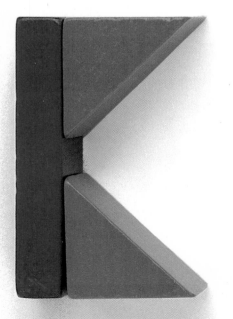

LEGO® is a registered trademark of INTERLEGO AG. The LEGO products shown are used with the special permission of the LEGO Group.

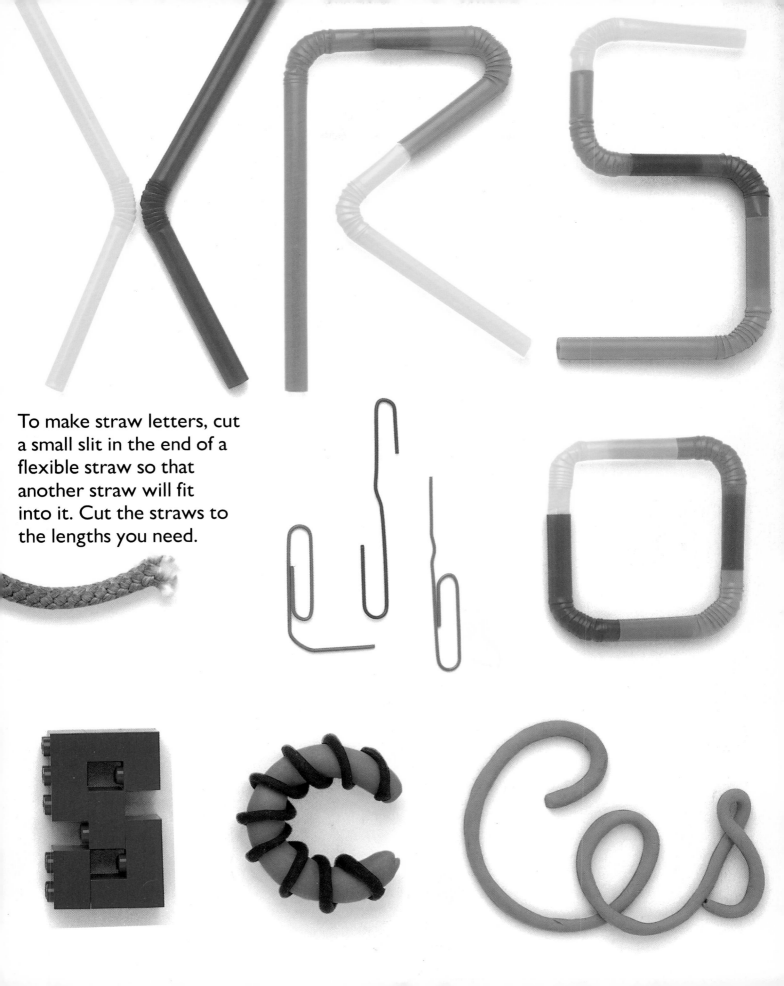

To make straw letters, cut
a small slit in the end of a
flexible straw so that
another straw will fit
into it. Cut the straws to
the lengths you need.

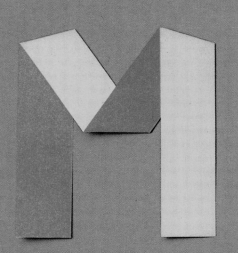

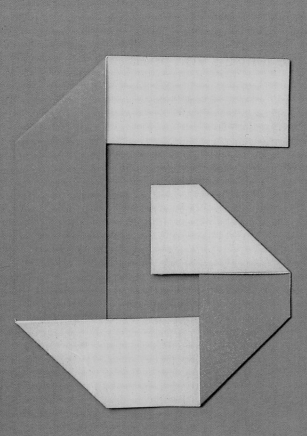

All the letters here were made by folding a single strip of paper. You could try gluing different colored strips of paper together so that the folds will show different colors.

First, experiment with some easy letters, such as the "T" here. Fold along the dotted lines as shown. Now try some of the other letters. With practice, you should be able to make a complete alphabet.

All these letters stand up on their own. The cardboard and balsa wood letters slot together; the wooden letters at the bottom of the page are glued together. Remember to make the slits exactly the same length so that they slot together neatly.

Ask a grown-up to cut some building blocks from a piece of wood. Paint them and arrange them to make letters.

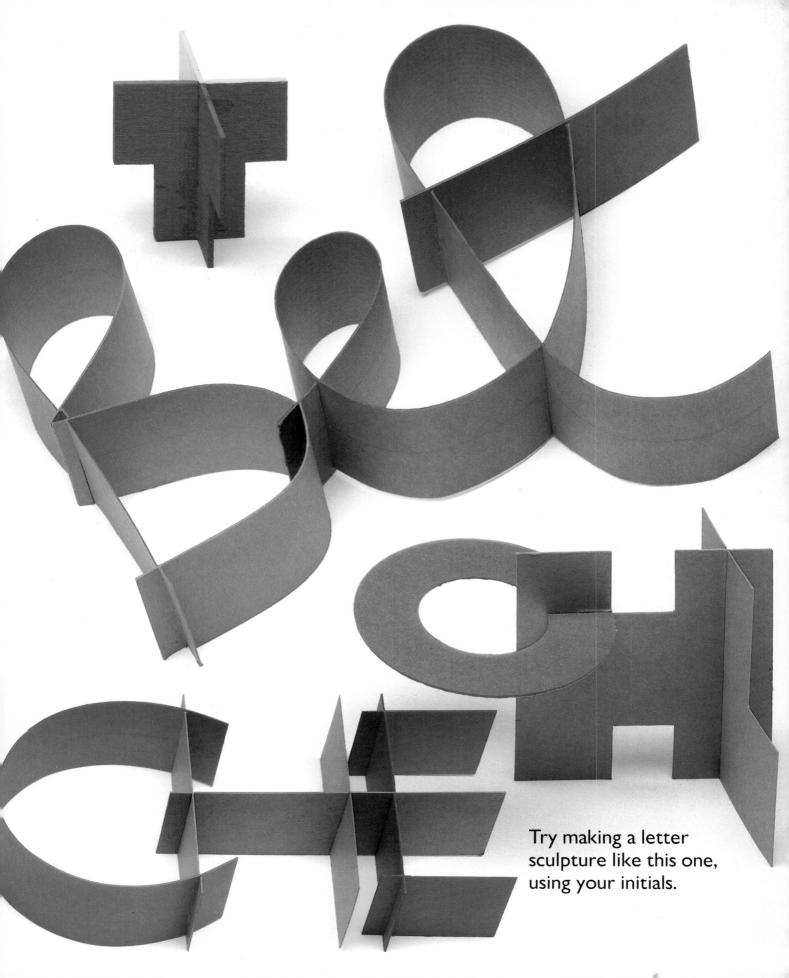

Try making a letter
sculpture like this one,
using your initials.

Try creating pop-up letters using folds and cuts to make them stand out from their background. Start with the pop-up "A" below as an experiment. The solid lines are cutting lines and the dotted lines are fold lines. Score along the dotted lines with a scoring tool – or the back of a pair of scissors – to make them easier to fold.

Another method for making pop-up letters is simply to add a long tab to the top and a short one to the bottom like the "D" and the "e" on the right. Fold a piece of paper in half and glue the tabs on.

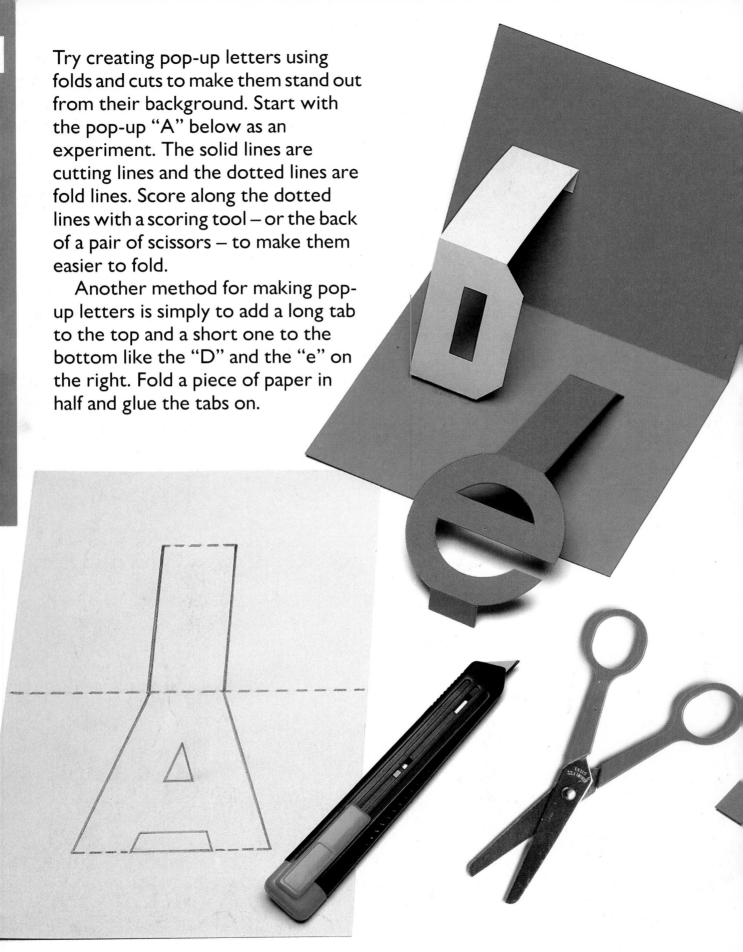

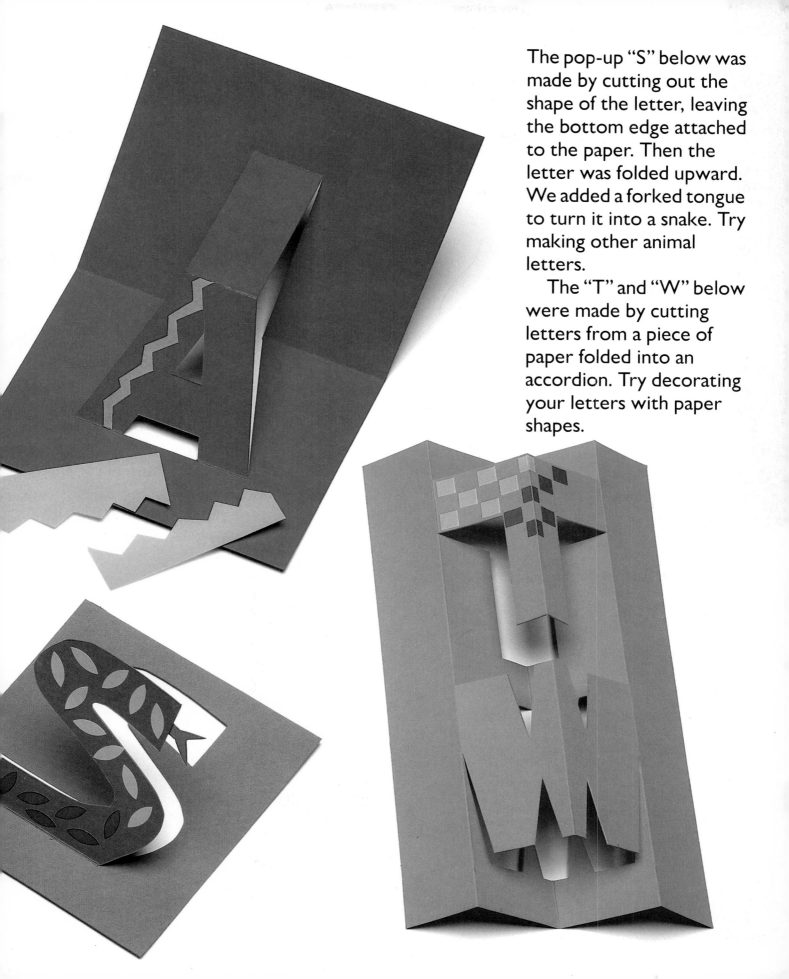

The pop-up "S" below was made by cutting out the shape of the letter, leaving the bottom edge attached to the paper. Then the letter was folded upward. We added a forked tongue to turn it into a snake. Try making other animal letters.

The "T" and "W" below were made by cutting letters from a piece of paper folded into an accordion. Try decorating your letters with paper shapes.

Printing and stenciling are good methods to use when you want to use letters more than once.

To make a potato-print letter, ask a grown-up to cut a potato in half and to cut the letter out of the potato so that it makes a raised surface to print from. Look for other objects, such as the erasers here, that can be used to print from. Simple shapes are best.

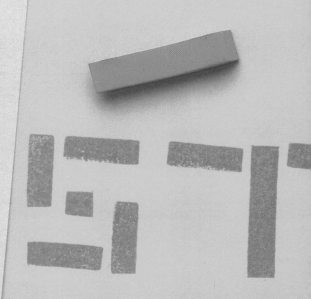

You may need help to cut stencils but it is useful to have a complete alphabet. Use stencil card which is durable. Keep the letters cut from the stencil card and try spattering paint over them, like the "E" at the top of the page. Use an old toothbrush or your finger and rub over the letter. You can also use a spray like the one on the equipment page. Use masking tape to keep your stencils in position without tearing the card.

Making patterns with letters is a good way to practice your printing and stenciling techniques and you can make some useful wrapping paper at the same time.

Try printing letters upside down and backward to make interesting shapes. Or try printing letters over other letters to make a new color. The letter pattern at the bottom right was made by using letters cut from magazines.

Here are some ideas for using letters to decorate bags, cards, badges, envelopes and writing paper. We used different techniques, such as printing, stenciling, cutting letters from colored paper and making letters from paper shapes. Try making your own writing paper or postcards using one of these techniques for your name.

Try making your own posters and shopping bags. Find a plain shopping bag or make one by using an existing bag as a pattern. Decorate with letters. Put your name or initials on your files and notebooks. On page 28 there are some ideas for designing letter pictures.

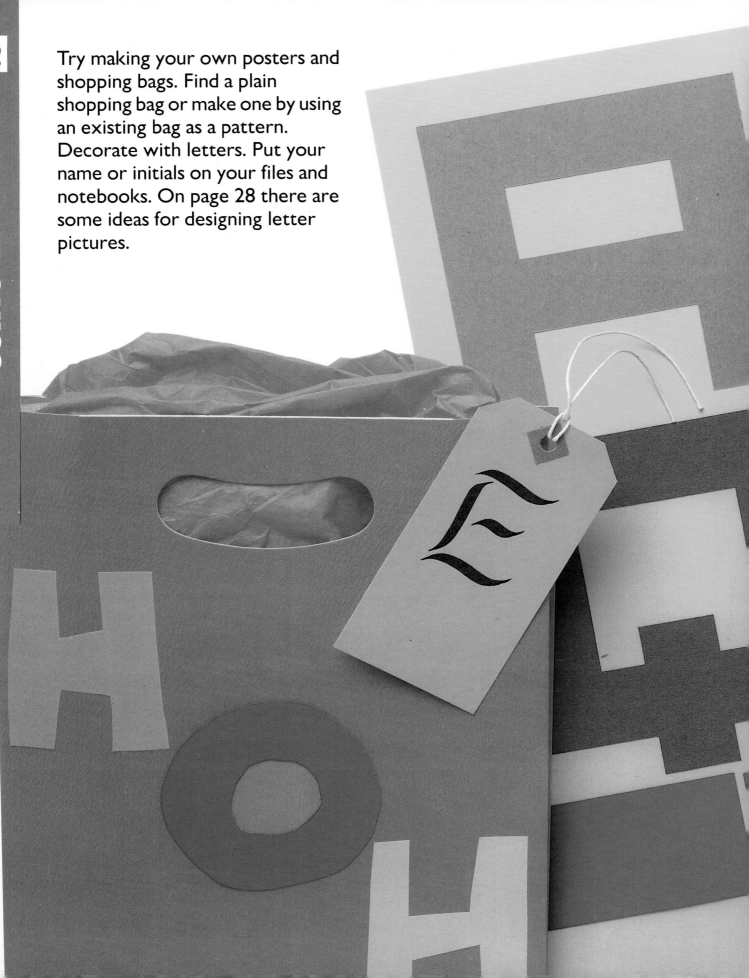

You can make letters from nearly anything – including food! Look for brightly colored candies with interesting shapes. Some candies and cookies are already made into letters.

Ask a grown-up to make some icing and put it into an icing bag. Squeeze the icing bag gently and make letters on cookies and cakes.

abcdefgh

All these letters were made using an italic pen or a brush with a flat end. First practice making simple strokes with an italic pen. Keep the nib at a 45° angle so that it makes thick and thin lines. When you start writing letters do not try to do a letter in one movement. Some letters need four or five strokes. Try using a brush with a flat end in the same way.

A

ivan
paris

GH

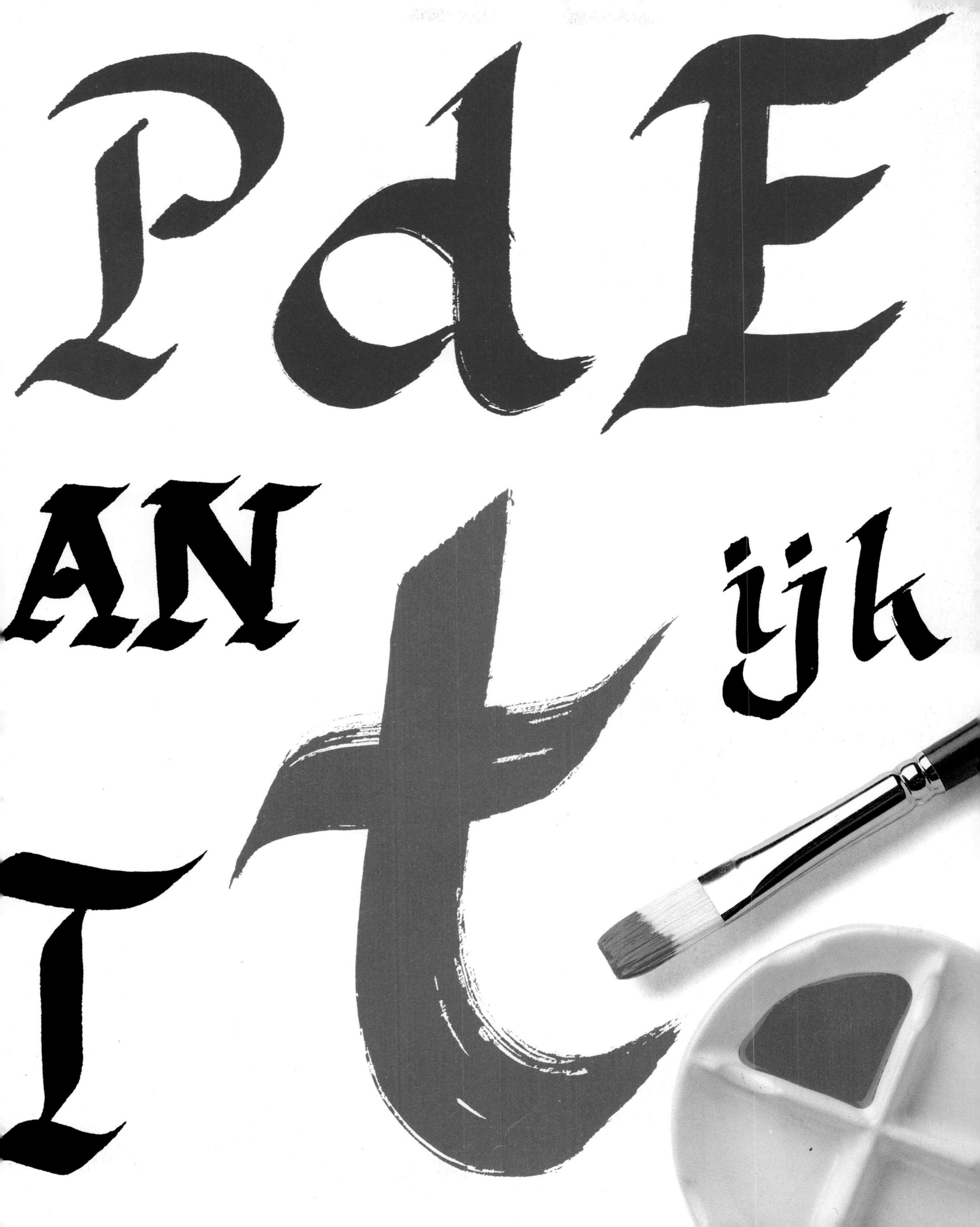
PdE
AN
ijk
T t

These jolly characters were made entirely from letters and numbers. Start a collection of letters cut from newspapers and magazines. Look for large letters from headlines and posters. Try putting different letters together to make pictures. When you are happy with the result, glue the letters onto paper or cardboard. Or you can use letter pictures to decorate your notebooks.

Here is an idea for personalizing your summer T-shirts and baseball caps.

Cut letters from brightly colored felt. You can stick on the letters with fabric glue. Or, if you are good at sewing, stitch them on with cotton or yarn, using big stitches.

These T-shirts are for special occasions because you will have to take the letters off before you wash them.

You can also paint letters on T-shirts using special fabric paints or pens.

Photograph of children by Fiona Pragoff